Your Nervous System

Alexander Lin

PICTURE CREDITS
Cover (front), Allsport Concepts/Getty Images; 1, 11 (bottom), 12 (bottom), Rubberball Productions/Getty Images Royalty-Free; 2-3, Jim Cummins/Corbis; 4-5 (top), 34 (bottom), Patrick Giardino/Corbis; 4-5 (bottom), 20 (top), 21, David Young-Wolff/PhotoEdit; 5 (top), Photodisc Blue/Getty Images Royalty-Free; 5 (bottom), 30 (top left), Comstock Images/Getty Images Royalty-Free; 7 (bottom), 9 (bottom), 15, 30 (top right), 34 (top), Photodisc Green/Getty Images Royalty-Free; 8, Amos Nachoum/Corbis; 10, JLP/Sylvia Torres/Corbis; 14 (top), David Stoecklein/Corbis; 16-17, Danny Lehman/Corbis; 18, Rick Doyle/Corbis; 20 (bottom), 23, John Henley/Corbis; 22 (left), Tim Klusalaas/Corbis; 22 (right), 31 (top left), Royalty-Free/Corbis; 25, 31 (bottom right), Stone/Getty Images; 26 (top), Brian J. Skerry/National Geographic Image Collection; 26 (bottom); Jim Zipp/Photo Researchers, Inc.; 27 (top), LWA-Dann Tardif/Corbis; 27 (bottom), Mark A. Johnson/Corbis; 28, Michael Newman/PhotoEdit; 29, Lester Lefkowitz/Corbis; 30 (bottom left and bottom right), Image 100/Getty Images Royalty-Free; 31 (top right), Roy McMahon/Corbis; 31 (middle left), Gabe Palmer/Corbis; 31 (middle right), John Turner/Corbis; 31 (bottom left), Tom & Dee Ann McCarthy/Corbis; 32, Brand X Pictures/Getty Images Royalty-Free.

Produced through the worldwide resources of the National Geographic Society, John M. Fahey, Jr., President and Chief Executive Officer; Gilbert M. Grosvenor, Chairman of the Board; Nina D. Hoffman, Executive Vice President and President, Books and Education Publishing Group.

PREPARED BY NATIONAL GEOGRAPHIC SCHOOL PUBLISHING
Ericka Markman, Senior Vice President and President, Children's Books and Education Publishing Group; Steve Mico, Senior Vice President, Editorial Director, Publisher; Francis Downey, Executive Editor; Richard Easby, Editorial Manager; Bea Jackson, Director of Layout and Design; Jim Hiscott, Design Manager; Cynthia Olson, Art Director; Margaret Sidlosky, Illustrations Director; Matt Wascavage, Manager of Publishing Services; Sean Philpotts, Jane Ponton, Production Managers; Ted Tucker, Production Specialist.

MANUFACTURING AND QUALITY CONTROL
Christopher A. Liedel, Chief Financial Officer; Phillip L. Schlosser, Director; Clifton M. Brown III, Manager

CONSULTANT AND REVIEWER
W. Michael Panneton, Professor of Pharmacological and Physiological Science, Saint Louis University School of Medicine

BOOK DEVELOPMENT
Amy Sarver

BOOK DESIGN/PHOTO RESEARCH
3R1 Group, Inc.

◄ **Your nervous system helps control how you move.**

Contents

Published by the National Geographic Society
1145 17th Street N.W.
Washington, D.C. 20036-4688

ISBN-13: 978-0-7922-5425-6
ISBN-10: 0-7922-5425-2

2012
  3 4 5 6 7 8 9 10 11 12 13 14 15

Printed in Canada.

A System That Controls

▲ **The nervous system helps you move.**

Think of all the things your body can do. You can talk to a friend. You can run. You can breathe while you are sleeping.

How does your body do all of these activities? You can do them because of your **nervous system**. This system controls many activities in the body.

Look at the pictures.

- What are the people doing in each picture?
- What activities does your nervous system help you do?

nervous system – the system that controls many activities in the body

▲ **The nervous system lets you talk to a friend.**

▲ The nervous system lets you think.

▲ The nervous system helps
you balance.

Big Idea
The nervous system helps control how your body works.

Set Purpose
Learn how the nervous system sends messages through your body.

Meet You

Your nervous system stretches from the top of your head to the tips of your toes. It even reaches inside your teeth and bones. The nervous system runs through almost every part of your body. It tells your body what to do.

The nervous system has three parts.
1. The brain
2. The spinal cord
3. Nerves

In this book, you will learn how the nervous system sends information through your body.

Questions You Will Explore

How does the nervous system work?

How does information get to and from the brain?

Nervous System

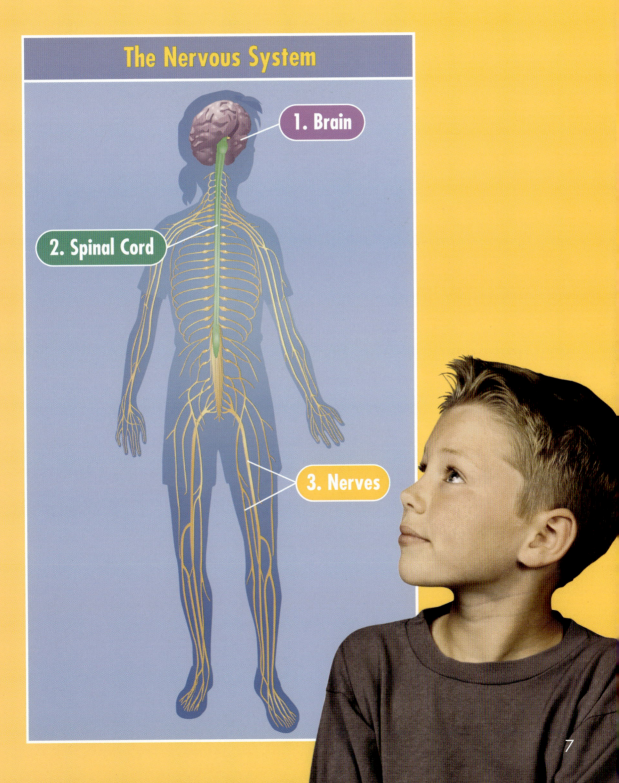

The Nervous System

1. Brain

2. Spinal Cord

3. Nerves

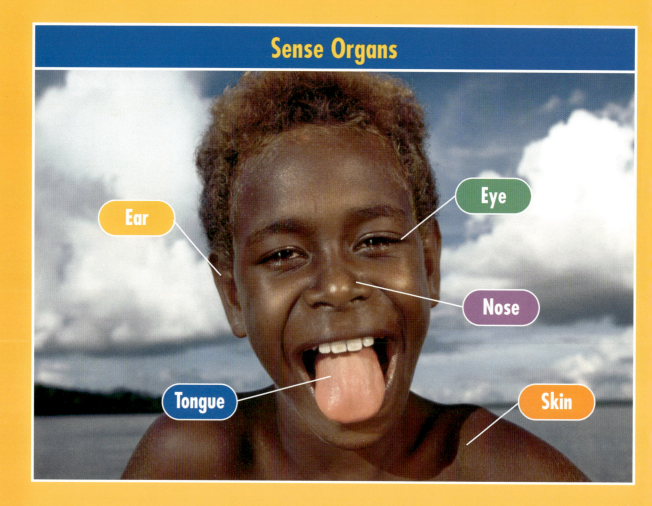

Labels on image: Ear, Eye, Nose, Tongue, Skin

Sensing the World

Your nervous system sends information about the world around you. Your body has sense organs that gather this information. Your eyes, ears, nose, skin, and tongue are all sense organs.

Each sense organ has special **cells**. Cells are tiny parts that make up your body. Cells work together to do jobs in your body. The cells in your sense organs give you information.

Eyes	**Sense light**
Ears	**Sense sound**
Nose	**Senses smell**
Skin	**Senses touch**
Tongue	**Senses taste**

cell – a tiny unit of a living thing

Tastes the Tongue Can Sense

Bitter

Sour

Salty

Sweet

How Sense Organs Work

Each of your sense organs does a different job. Let's take a closer look at the sense organs on the tongue. These sense organs are called **taste buds.** Taste buds sense different tastes.

These tastes are sweet, sour, salty, and bitter. When you eat, your taste buds pick up information about these tastes. They send this information to the brain.

taste bud – a part of your tongue that senses taste

▼ Taste buds sense the taste of food.

The Brain Gives Meaning

You get information about the world through your sense organs. Yet it is your brain that gives meaning to all of that information. Suppose you eat a piece of fruit. Your taste buds get information about the fruit. The brain uses that information to tell you that the fruit is sweet.

Some Parts of the Brain

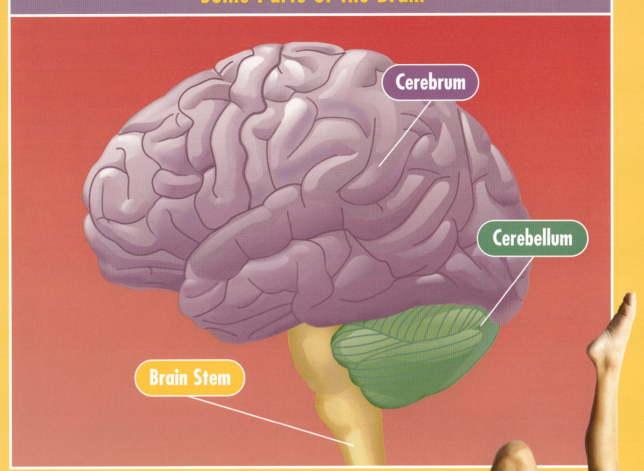

Cerebrum

Cerebellum

Brain Stem

Your Body's Control Center

Your brain is the command center of the nervous system. Your brain has parts that are in charge of different activities.

- Cerebrum: Gives meaning to sense information and lets you think, learn, and remember
- Cerebellum: Helps control movement
- Brain Stem: Controls breathing and other activities

Your brain controls just about everything in your body.

▶ Your cerebellum gives you balance.

11

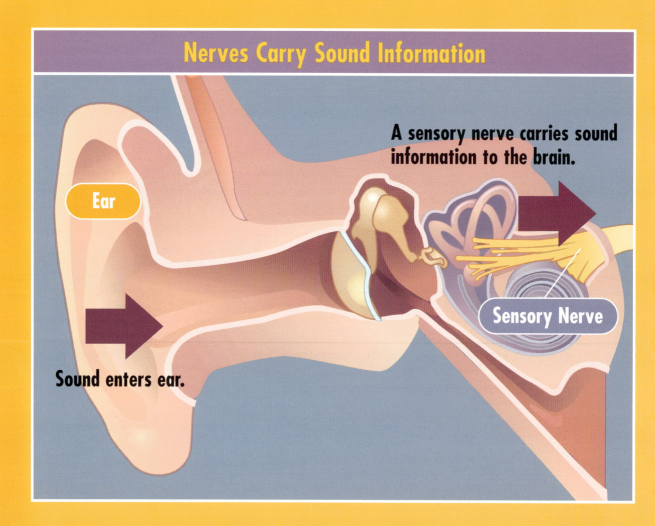

Nerves Carry Sound Information

Ear

A sensory nerve carries sound information to the brain.

Sound enters ear.

Sensory Nerve

Nerves at Work

So how does information get to and from your brain? Nerve cells carry the messages.

Suppose you turn on a radio. Your ears take in sound. Then the sound is passed into the brain along a nerve cell. Nerve cells that carry messages to the brain are called **sensory nerves**. Sensory nerves give the brain the information from your ears. The brain makes sense of the information. It understands the sounds as music.

sensory nerve – a nerve cell that carries messages to the brain from the rest of the body

Nerve Cells Carry Messages

Nerve Cell

A message travels along the nerve cell.

The message jumps to another nerve cell.

Nerve Cell

▲ A message travels through the body by jumping from one nerve cell to another.

Nerves Pass Information

Sensory nerves take information to the brain. **Motor nerves** take information from the brain to the rest of the body. How does this information travel through the body?

The messages to and from the brain pass from nerve cell to nerve cell. Yet the cells do not touch each other. Messages jump from nerve cell to nerve cell.

motor nerve – a nerve cell that carries messages from the brain to the rest of the body

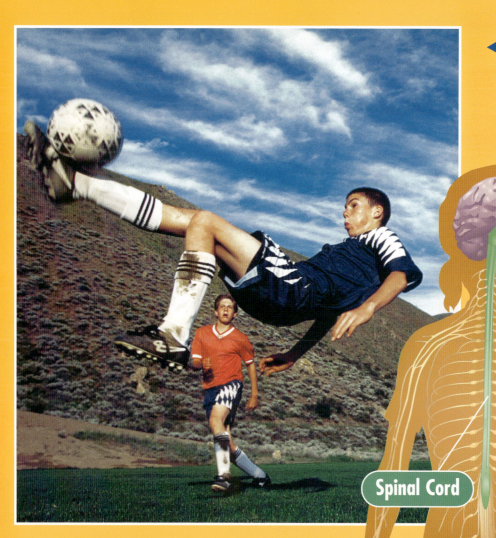

◀ Messages between the feet and brain travel along nerves into and out of the spinal cord.

Brain

Spinal Cord

Nerves

The Spinal Cord Connection

Messages from your ear to your brain do not have far to travel. That is not the case for messages from your hands and feet. They have a long way to go to reach the brain. So messages travel along nerves into and out of the spinal cord.

The spinal cord is an important part of the nervous system. It connects your brain to the rest of the body. It is the main link that takes messages to and from your brain.

▲ The parts of your nervous system work together to keep you safe when crossing the street.

A System That Works Together

Your brain, spinal cord, and nerves are always passing along information. Think about walking across a street. Your eyes look for cars. Sensory nerves carry this information to your brain. Your brain decides if it is safe to cross the street. When it is safe, the brain sends a message. The spinal cord and motor nerves carry the message to your feet. Then you walk across the street.

The parts of your nervous system are always working together. They help you make sense of the world.

Stop and Think!

How do messages travel through your nervous system?

15

Recap

Explain how the nervous system sends messages through your body.

Set Purpose

Learn how nerves in your skin help to keep you safe.

A To

A butterfly lands on your hand. How do you feel such a lightweight thing? It is your sense of touch. This sense really keeps you informed about yourself and the world around you.

uchy Subject

▲ **Skin covers and protects your body.**

Your Amazing Skin

Your sense of touch comes from your skin. The skin is the body's biggest organ. Skin weighs about three kilograms (six pounds). If you spread out your skin, it would be about the size of a bedsheet!

Your skin is big for a reason. It covers and protects your body. Skin helps keep your body at the right temperature. Skin is also the sense organ that lets you feel things.

Beneath the Surface

Look at your body. The skin you see is just the top layer. This layer of skin is made of dead skin cells. These dead cells protect your body.

Below the surface is where your living skin cells are found. The nerves that let you feel things are here. These nerves have **receptors** that sense temperature and pain. They also have receptors that sense pressure or touch. There are millions of receptors in your skin!

receptor – a nerve ending that can sense temperature, pain, and pressure

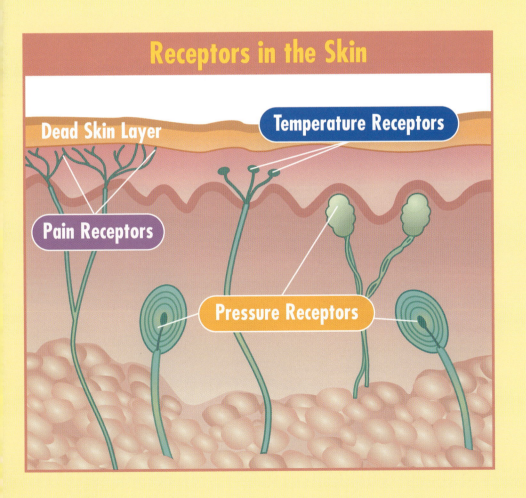

Receptors in the Skin

Dead Skin Layer

Temperature Receptors

Pain Receptors

Pressure Receptors

From Skin to Brain

The receptors in the skin gather information about things you touch. Nerves then carry these messages to your brain. Some receptors sense temperature. If you touch an ice cube, receptors sense cold. If you touch a warm bowl of soup, they sense warmth.

Temperature receptors sometimes stop sensing temperature. This can happen when a receptor gets the same information for a long time. Think about getting into a hot bath. At first the water feels hot. But after a few minutes your body gets used to it. Your receptors stop sending the hot message. Then you do not notice the water is hot.

▲ Receptors in your skin sense that an ice cube is cold.

▼ After being in a hot bath for a few minutes, your receptors stop sending messages about the water temperature.

▲ Pain receptors let you know if something is sharp, such as the spines of a cactus.

Pain and Pressure

Your skin also has other kinds of receptors. Some sense pain. Your pain receptors help keep your body safe. They let you know if something is sharp or too hot.

Some receptors can also sense pressure, or touch. Some pressure receptors are near the top layer of your skin. They can pick up a gentle pressure, such as a fly landing on your arm. Some pressure receptors are deep in your skin. These pick up a strong pressure, such as the pressure of sitting on a hard bench.

Sweat and Shivers

Receptors sense information. They send this information to the brain along nerves. Yet sometimes your brain sends out messages to your skin. This happens when your body gets hot. If you get hot, your brain sends messages to the sweat glands in your skin. Sweat glands are parts of your skin that make sweat. Soon your skin is covered with sweat. The sweat helps cool your body.

▼ When you get hot, your nervous system tells your body to make sweat to cool you.

Your brain also sends messages to your skin when it is cold. Your brain tells muscles in your skin to shiver. You shiver when these muscles tighten and loosen quickly. This can warm your body.

▲ When you are cold, your nervous system tells your body to shiver for warmth.

Your skin and nervous system work together to make sense of the world around you.

Skin and the Nervous System

Your skin and nervous system work together in many ways. Your skin's receptors give you your sense of touch. Your brain uses that information to keep you safe. Your brain also sends messages to the skin to keep your body working well. Your skin and nervous system help you stay in touch with your world!

Stop and Think!

How do the nerves in your skin help keep you safe?

Recap
Describe how your sense of touch helps keep you safe.

Set Purpose
Read these articles to learn more about senses and your nervous system.

Your Nervous System

Your nervous system does many important jobs in your body. Here are some things you learned about your nervous system.

- The nervous system is made of your brain, spinal cord, and nerves.
- Your nervous system gets information from your sense organs.
- Nerves carry messages to and from the brain.
- Your brain gives meaning to information and sends messages to your body.

Check What You Have Learned

How do your nervous system and your sense organs work together?

▲ Your nose contains sense organs that connect to the brain along nerves.

Super Animals

Some animals have super sense organs. Sharks have a very good sense of smell. Many can smell blood in the water from far away.

Some animals have great eyesight. A red-tailed hawk flies high in the air. But it can still spot a tiny mouse moving on the ground far below.

▼ **Shark**

▼ **Red-tailed hawk**

◀ A helmet protects your head while you play baseball.

Brain Safety

Your brain is a very important part of your body. So it needs protection. The hard bones of your skull help do the job. But sometimes they are not enough.

Do you want to protect your head? Then wear a helmet when you play sports or ride your bike. A helmet will help to keep your head safe.

▶ A bike helmet can protect your brain when you ride a bike.

Brainy Exercise

You know exercise is good for your body. Now researchers say it may help your brain, too.

New studies say that older people who exercise do better on certain kinds of tests. This may also be true for kids. One study found that very fit kids did better on some tests. So now you can exercise for both a good body and a good brain!

▼ Exercise is good for your body and your brain.

▲ A neuroscientist studies the nervous system.

Answering Future Questions

There has never been a better time to be a neuroscientist. A neuroscientist studies the nervous system.

There are many exciting questions that neuroscientists try to answer. Will we be able to fix injured spinal cords? How can we better stop pain?

You have to study and work hard to become a neuroscientist. But it is a very rewarding job.

Many kinds of words are used in this book. Here you will learn about antonyms. You will also learn about multiple-meaning words.

Antonyms

Antonyms are words that have opposite meanings. Find the antonyms below. Use each antonym in your own sentence.

Receptors in your skin can sense that an ice cube is **cold.**

Receptors in your skin can sense that the soup is **hot.**

They walk **to** the car.

They run **away** from the car.

Multiple-Meaning Words

A multiple-meaning word is a word that has more than one meaning. Find the multiple-meaning words below. Then use each word in your own sentence.

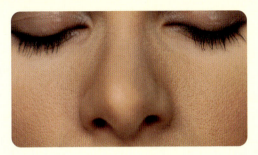

The nose is a sense **organ.**

She plays the **organ.**

He takes **charge** and finds the answer to the problem.

He uses a credit card to **charge** his purchase.

They **pass** the message by whispering.

She uses her **pass** to board the airplane.

Research and Write

Write About Taste

Research the sense receptors on your tongue. Find out about the four main tastes your tongue can sense: bitter, sour, sweet, and salty. Then write about what you learned.

Research

Get a salted pretzel, a lemon, a marshmallow, and a piece of unsweetened chocolate. Taste each food. Touch each food to the front, sides, and back of your tongue as you taste it.

Take Notes

As you taste each food, take notes. Tell how each food tasted.

Write

Make a chart. List the foods you tasted and tell which of the four main tastes each one had. Explain how the nervous system helped you understand the different tastes of the foods.

Read More About the Nervous System

Find and read other books about the nervous system and your body. As you read, think about these questions.

- Why is the nervous system important to your body?
- How does the nervous system work with other parts of your body?
- How do scientists learn about the nervous system?

Books to Read

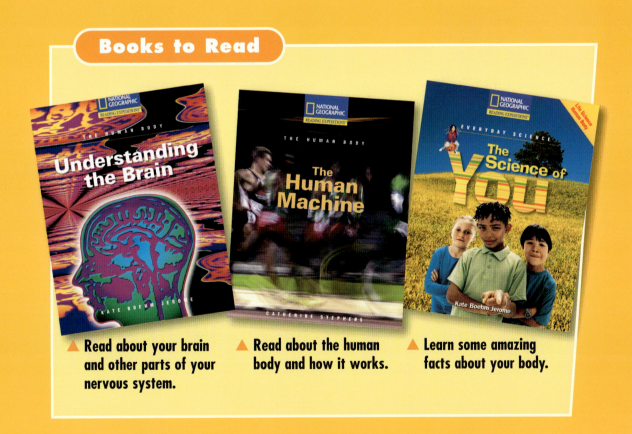

▲ Read about your brain and other parts of your nervous system.

▲ Read about the human body and how it works.

▲ Learn some amazing facts about your body.

Glossary

KEY CONCEPT

cell (page 8)
A tiny unit of a living thing
Cells on your tongue take in taste information.

KEY CONCEPT

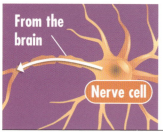

From the brain

Nerve cell

motor nerve (page 13)
A nerve cell that carries messages from the brain
to the rest of the body
You smile when motor nerves carry messages from your
brain to the muscles around your mouth.

KEY CONCEPT

nervous system (page 4)
The system that controls many activities in the body
Your nervous system is made of the brain, spinal cord,
and nerves.

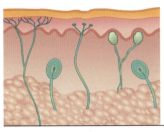

receptor (page 19)

A nerve ending that can sense temperature, pain, and pressure

Receptors in your skin give you the sense of touch.

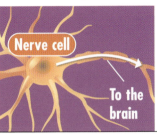

sensory nerve (page 12)

A nerve cell that carries messages to the brain from the rest of the body

Sensory nerves on your tongue send information about taste to your brain.

Nerve cell

To the brain

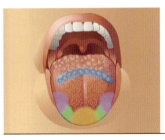

taste bud (page 9)

A part of your tongue that senses taste

A taste bud can sense bitter, sweet, salty, or sour tastes.

Index